HONEST TO GOD:
Prayer for Every Day

A four-week course to help people make
prayer a part of their daily lives.

by
Bob Buller

Apply·It·To·Life™

Adult

BIBLE CURRICULUM
from Group

Group
Loveland, Colorado

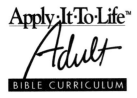

Group

Honest to God: Prayer for Every Day
Copyright © 1996 Group Publishing, Inc.

Credits
Contributing Author: Walt Sampson
Senior Editor: Paul Woods
Creative Products Director: Joani Schultz
Art Directors: Kathy Benson and Helen H. Lannis
Cover Designer: Liz Howe
Cover Illustrator: Joel Armstrong
Illustrator: Rex Bohn

ISBN 1-55945-518-7

10 9 8 7 6 5 4 3 2 1   05 04 03 02 01 00 99 98 97 96

Printed in the United States of America.

C O N T E N T S

INTRODUCTION   5

What Is Apply-It-To-Life™ Adult Bible Curriculum?   5
What Makes Apply-It-To-Life Adult Bible Curriculum Unique?   5
How to Use Apply-It-To-Life Adult Bible Curriculum   9
Course Introduction—Honest to God: Prayer for Every Day   11
Publicity Page   13

LESSON 1   15

Straight From the Heart
Prayer is more a moment-by-moment attitude than a momentary act.

LESSON 2   27

The Right Answer Every Time
God answers each prayer with wisdom and love.

LESSON 3   39

Praying When Life Is Bad
We can approach God with our innermost feelings and most urgent needs.

LESSON 4   51

Praying When Life Is Good
We honor God with honest praise and open thanks.

FELLOWSHIP AND OUTREACH SPECIALS   63

Introduction

WHAT IS APPLY-IT-TO-LIFE™ ADULT BIBLE CURRICULUM?

Apply-It-To-Life™ Adult Bible Curriculum is a series of four-week study courses designed to help you facilitate powerful lessons that will help class members grow in faith. Use this course with

- Sunday school classes,
- home study groups,
- weekday Bible study groups,
- men's Bible studies,
- women's Bible studies, and
- family classes.

The variety of courses gives the adult student a broad coverage of topical, life-related issues and significant biblical topics. In addition, as the name of the series implies, every lesson helps the adult student apply Scripture to his or her life.

Each course in Apply-It-To-Life Adult Bible Curriculum provides four lessons on different aspects of one topic. In each course, you also receive Fellowship and Outreach Specials connected to the month's topic. They provide outreach activities, suggestions for building closer relationships in your class, and even a party idea!

WHAT MAKES APPLY-IT-TO-LIFE™ ADULT BIBLE CURRICULUM UNIQUE?

Teaching as Jesus Taught

Jesus was a master teacher. With Apply-It-To-Life Adult Bible Curriculum, you'll use the same teaching methods and principles that Jesus used:

- **Active Learning.** Think back on an important lesson you've learned in life. Did you learn it from reading about it? from hearing about it? from something you did? Chances are, the most important lessons you've learned came from things you experienced. That's what active learning is—learning by doing. Active learning leads students through activities and experiences that help them understand important principles, messages, and ideas. It's a discovery process that helps people internalize and remember what they learn.

Jesus often used active learning. One of the most vivid examples is his washing of his disciples' feet. In Apply-It-To-Life Adult Bible Curriculum, the teacher might remove his or her shoes and socks, then read aloud the foot-washing passage from John 13, or the teacher might choose to actually wash people's feet. Participants won't soon forget it. Active learning uses simple activities to teach profound lessons.

● **Interactive Learning.** Interactive learning means learning through small-group interaction and discussion. Each person is actively involved in discovering God's truth. Interactive learning puts people in pairs, trios, or foursomes to involve everyone in the learning experience. It takes active learning a step further by having people who have gone through an experience teach others what they've learned.

Jesus often helped cement the learning from an experience by questioning people—sometimes in small groups—about what had happened. He regularly questioned his followers and his opponents, forcing them to think and to discuss among themselves what he was teaching them. After washing his disciples' feet, the first thing Jesus did was ask the disciples if they understood what he had done. After the foot-washing activity, the teacher might form small groups and have people discuss how they felt when the leader removed his or her shoes and socks. Then group members might compare those feelings and the learning involved to what the disciples must have experienced.

● **Biblical Depth.** Apply-It-To-Life Adult Bible Curriculum recognizes that most people are ready to go below the surface to better understand the deeper truths of the Bible. Therefore, the activities and studies go beyond an "easy answer" approach to Christian education and lead people to grapple with difficult issues from a biblical perspective.

In the Bible Basis, you'll find information that will help you understand the Scriptures you're dealing with. Within the class-time section of the lesson, thought-provoking activities and discussions lead adults to new depths of biblical understanding. "Bible Insights" within the lesson give pertinent information that will bring the Bible to life for you and your class members. In-class handouts give adults significant Bible information and challenge them to search for and discover biblical truths for themselves. Finally, the "For Even Deeper Discussion" sections provide questions that will lead your class members to new and deeper levels of insight and application.

No one questions the depth of Jesus' teachings or the effectiveness of his teaching methods. This curriculum follows Jesus' example and helps people probe the depths of the Bible in a way no other adult curriculum does.

● **Bible Application.** Jesus didn't stop with helping people understand truth. It wasn't enough that the rich young ruler knew all the right answers. Jesus wanted him to take action on what he knew. In the same way, Apply-It-To-Life Adult Bible Curriculum encourages a response in people's lives. That's why this curriculum is called "Apply-It-To-Life"! Depth of understanding means little if the truths of Scripture don't zing into people's hearts. Each lesson brings home one point and encourages people to consider the changes they might make in response.

● **One Purpose.** In each study, every activity works toward communicating and applying the same point. People may discover other new truths, but the study doesn't load them down with a mass of information. Sometimes less is more. When lessons try to teach too much, they often fail to teach anything. Even Jesus limited his teaching to what he felt people could really learn and apply (John 16:12). Apply-It-To-Life Adult Bible Curriculum makes sure that class members thoroughly understand and apply one point each week.

● **Variety.** Jesus constantly varied his teaching methods. One day he would have a serious discussion with his disciples about who he was, and another day he'd baffle them by turning water into wine. What he didn't do was allow them to become bored with what he had to teach them.

Any kind of study can become less than exciting if the leader and students do everything the same way week after week. Apply-It-To-Life Adult Bible Curriculum varies activities and approaches to keep everyone's interest level high each week. In one class, you might have people in small groups "put themselves in the disciples' sandals" and experience something of the confusion of Jesus' death and resurrection. In another lesson, class members may experience problems in communication and examine how such problems can damage relationships.

● **Relevance.** People today want to know how to live successfully right now. They struggle with living as authentic Christians at work, in the family, and in the community. They want to know how the Bible can help them live faithful lives—how it can help them face the difficulties of living in today's culture. Apply-It-To-Life Adult Bible Curriculum bridges the gap between biblical truth and the "real world" issues of people's lives. Jesus didn't discuss with his followers the eschatological significance of Ezekiel's wheels, and Apply-It-To-Life Adult Bible Curriculum won't either! Courses and studies in this curriculum focus on the real needs of people and help them discover answers in Scripture that will help meet those needs.

● **A Nonthreatening Atmosphere.** In many adult classes, people feel intimidated because they're new Christians or because they don't have the Bible knowledge they think they should have. Jesus sometimes intimidated those who opposed him, but he consistently treated his followers with understanding and respect. We want people in church to experience the same understanding and respect Jesus' followers experienced. With Apply-It-To-Life Adult Bible Curriculum, no one is embarrassed for not knowing or understanding as much as someone else. In fact, the interactive learning process minimizes the differences between those with vast Bible knowledge and those with little Bible knowledge. Lessons often begin with nonthreatening, sharing questions and move slowly toward more depth. Whatever their level of knowledge or commitment, class members will work together to discover biblical truths that can affect their lives.

● **A Group That Cares.** Jesus chose 12 people who learned from him together. That group practically lived together—sharing one another's hurts, joys, and ambitions. Sometimes Jesus divided the 12 into smaller groups and worked with just three or four at a time.

Adults today long for a close-knit group with whom they can share personal needs and joys. Activities in this curriculum will help class members get to know one another better and care for one another more as they study the Bible and apply its truths to their lives. As people reveal their thoughts and feelings to one another, they'll grow closer and develop more commitment to the group. And they'll be encouraging one another along the way!

● **An Element of Delight.** We don't often think about Jesus' ministry in this way, but he often brought fun and delight to his followers. Remember the time he raised Peter's mother-in-law or the time he sat happily with children on his lap? How about the joy and excitement at his triumphal entry into Jerusalem or the time he helped his disciples catch a boatload of fish—after they'd fished all night with no success?

People learn more when they're having fun. So within Apply-It-To-Life Adult Bible Curriculum, elements of fun and delight pop up often. And sometimes adding fun is as simple as using a carrot for a pretend microphone!

Taking the Fear out of Teaching

Teachers love Apply-It-To-Life Adult Bible Curriculum because it makes teaching much less stressful. Lessons in this curriculum...

● **are easy to teach.** Interactive learning frees the teacher from being a dispenser of information to serve as a facilitator of learning. Teachers can spend class time guiding people to discover and apply biblical truths. The studies provide clear, understandable Bible background; easy-to-prepare learning experiences; and thought-provoking discussion questions.

● **can be prepared quickly.** Lessons in Apply-It-To-Life Adult Bible Curriculum are logical and clear. There's no sorting through tons of information to figure out the lesson. In 30 minutes, a busy teacher can easily read a lesson and prepare to teach it. In addition, optional and For Extra Time activities allow the teacher to tailor the lesson to the class. And the thorough instructions and questions will guide even an inexperienced teacher through each powerful lesson.

● **let everyone share in the class' success.** With Apply-It-To-Life Adult Bible Curriculum, the teacher is one of the participants. The teacher still guides the class, but the burden is not as heavy. Everyone participates and adds to the study's effectiveness. So when the study has an impact, everyone shares in that success.

● **lead the teacher to new discoveries.** Each lesson is designed to help the teacher first discover a biblical truth. And most teachers will make additional discoveries as they prepare each lesson. In class, the teacher will discover even more as other adults share what they have found. As with any type of teaching, the teacher will likely learn more than anyone else in the class!

● **provide relevant information to class members.** Photocopiable handouts are designed to help people better understand or interpret Bible passages. And the handouts make teaching easier because the teacher can often refer to them for small-group discussion questions and instructions.

First familiarize yourself with an Apply-It-To-Life Adult Bible Curriculum lesson. The following explanations will help you understand how the lesson elements work together.

Lesson Elements

● The **Opening** maps out the lesson's agenda and introduces the topic for the session. Sometimes this activity will help people get better acquainted as they begin to explore the topic together.

● The **Bible Exploration and Application** activities will help people discover what the Bible says about the topic and how the lesson's point applies to their lives. In these varied activities, class members find answers to the "So what?" question. They discover the relevance of the Scriptures and commit to growing closer to God.

You may use one or both of the options in this section. They are designed to stand alone or to work together. Both present the same point in different ways. "For Even Deeper Discussion" questions appear at the end of each activity in this section. Use these questions whenever you feel they might be particularly helpful for your class.

● The **Closing** pulls everything in the lesson together and often funnels the lesson's message into a time of reflection and prayer.

● The **For Extra Time** section is just that. Use it when you've completed the lesson and still have time left or when you've used one Bible Exploration and Application option and don't have time to do the other. Or you might plan to use it instead of another option.

When you put all the sections together, you get a lesson that's fun and easy to teach. Plus, participants will learn truths they'll remember and apply to their daily lives.

Guidelines for a Successful Adult Class

● **Be a facilitator, not a lecturer.** Your job is to direct the activities and facilitate the discussions. You become a choreographer of sorts: someone who gets everyone else involved in the discussion and keeps the discussion on track.

● **Teach adults how to form small groups.** Help adults form groups of four, three, or two—whatever the activity calls for. Small-group sharing allows for more discussion and involvement by all participants. It's not as threatening or scary to open up to two people as it would be to 20 or 200!

Some leaders decide not to form small groups because they want to hear everybody's ideas. The intention is good, but some people just won't talk in a large group. Use a "report back" time after small-group discussions to gather the best responses from all groups.

Try creative group-forming methods to help everyone in the class get to know one another. For example, have class members form groups with others who are wearing the same color, shop at the same grocery store, were born the same month, or like the same season of the year.

● **Encourage relationship building.** George Barna, in his insightful book about the church, *The Frog in the Kettle,* explains that adults today have a strong need to develop friendships. In a society of high-tech toys, "personal" computers, and lonely commutes, people long for positive human contact. That's where our church classes and groups can jump in. Help adults form friendships through your class. What's discovered in a classroom setting will be better applied when friends support each other outside the classroom. In fact, the relationships begun in your class may be as important as the truths you help your adults learn.

● **Expect the unexpected.** Active learning is an adventure that doesn't always take you where you think you're going. Be open to the different directions the Holy Spirit may lead your class. When something goes wrong or an unexpected emotion is aroused, take advantage of this teachable moment. Ask probing questions; follow up on someone's deep need.

What should you do if people go off on a tangent? Don't panic. People learn best when they're engaged in meaningful discussion. And if you get through even one activity, your class will discover the point for the whole lesson. So relax. It's OK if you don't get everything done.

● **Participate—and encourage participation.** Apply-It-To-Life Adult Bible Curriculum is only as interactive as you and your class make it. Jump into discussions yourself, but don't "take over." Encourage everyone to participate. Use "active listening" responses such as rephrasing and summing up what's been said. To get more out of your discussions, use follow-up inquiries such as "Can you tell me more?" "What do you mean by that?" or "What makes you feel that way?" The more people participate, the more they'll discover God's truths for themselves.

● **Trust the Holy Spirit.** All the previous guidelines and the instructions in the lessons will be irrelevant if you ignore the presence of God in your classroom. God sent the Holy Spirit as our helper. As you use this curriculum, ask the Holy Spirit to help you facilitate the lessons. And ask the Holy Spirit to direct your class toward God's truth. Trust that God's Spirit can work through each person's discoveries, not just the teacher's.

How to Use This Course

Before the Four-Week Session
● Read the Course Introduction and This Course at a Glance (pp. 11-12).

● Decide how you'll use the art on the Publicity Page (p. 13) to publicize the course. Prepare fliers, newsletter articles, and posters as needed.

● Look at the Fellowship and Outreach Specials (pp. 63-64) and decide which ones you'll use.

Before Each Lesson
● Read the one-sentence Point, the Objectives, and the Bible Basis for the lesson. The Bible Basis provides background information on the lesson's passages and shows how those passages relate to people today.

- Choose which activities you'll use from the lesson. Remember—it's not necessary to do every activity. Pick the ones that best fit your group and your time allotment.
- Gather necessary supplies and make photocopies of any handouts you intend to use. They're listed in This Lesson at a Glance.
- Read each section of the lesson. Adjust activities as necessary to fit your class size and meeting room, but be careful not to delete all the activity. People learn best when they're actively involved.
- Make one photocopy of the "Apply-It-To-Life This Week!" handout for each class member.

COURSE INTRODUCTION— HONEST TO GOD: PRAYER FOR EVERY DAY

According to researcher George Barna, "Americans may be the most prayerful people on earth" (*Absolute Confusion* [Ventura, CA: Regal Books, 1993], p. 103). Nine out of 10 American adults claim to pray from time to time, while 58 percent say they pray every day. In addition, 82 percent of the Americans who pray do so regularly and not just in crisis situations. Finally, 79 percent of the people Barna surveyed believe to some degree that prayer makes a real difference in their lives (pp. 94-96).

In spite of these positive signs, Barna reports that there's still significant room for improvement. The average adult prayer is about five minutes long (p. 96) and thus falls considerably short of Paul's ideal of unceasing prayer (1 Thessalonians 5:17). In addition, only 26 percent of American adults are entirely satisfied with the quality of their prayer lives (p. 94). Presumably the other 74 percent would like to pray more regularly or more effectively but need someone to show them how.

That's where this course comes in. Using the activities and resources that follow, you can help "the 74 percent" in your class make prayer a natural and vital part of their daily lives. At the same time, you can lead those who are already satisfied with their prayer lives into an even deeper and more meaningful experience of conversation and communion with God.

This four-week course will help you achieve these lofty goals by showing how the proper attitude of prayer promotes regular and meaningful acts of prayer. In addition, class members will increase their faith in God when they learn that every answer to prayer—including "no" and "not now"—is an expression of God's goodness and wisdom. Finally, people will approach God with increased confidence and honesty when they discover the biblical models for praying when life is bad as well as when it's good. By the time they complete this course, your class members will be ready and eager to be "honest to God" every moment of every day for the rest of their lives.

This Course at a Glance

Before you dive into the lessons, familiarize yourself with each lesson's point. Then read the Scripture passages.
- Study them to gain insight into the lessons.
- Use them as a basis for your personal devotions.
- Think about how they relate to people's situations today.

Lesson 1: Straight From the Heart
The Point: Prayer is more a moment-by-moment attitude than a momentary act.
Bible Basis: Romans 8:26-27; Ephesians 6:18; and 1 Thessalonians 5:17

Lesson 2: The Right Answer Every Time
The Point: God answers each prayer with wisdom and love.
Bible Basis: Matthew 7:7-11 and 2 Corinthians 12:1-10

Lesson 3: Praying When Life Is Bad
The Point: We can approach God with our innermost feelings and most urgent needs.
Bible Basis: Psalms 6:1-10; 39:1-13; and 143:1-12

Lesson 4: Praying When Life Is Good
The Point: We honor God with honest praise and open thanks.
Bible Basis: James 5:13; Psalms 30:1-12; and 113:1-9

Grab your congregation's attention! Add the vital details to the ready-made flier below, photocopy it, and use it to advertise this course on prayer. Insert the flier in your bulletins. Enlarge it to make posters. Splash the art or anything else from this page in newsletters, in bulletins, or even on postcards! It's that simple.

*The art from this page is also available on Group's MinistryNet™ computer on-line resource for you to manipulate on your computer. Call **800-447-1070** for information.*

HONEST TO GOD — PRAYER · FOR · EVERY · DAY ·

A FOUR-WEEK ADULT COURSE ON PRAYING REGULARLY AND EFFECTIVELY.

C O M E   T O

O N

A T

COME EXPLORE HOW TO MAKE PRAYER AN IMPORTANT PART OF YOUR DAILY LIFE!

Apply·It·To·Life™
Adult
BIBLE CURRICULUM
from **Group**

PRAYER · FOR · EVERY · DAY ·

HONEST TO GOD

Straight From the Heart

Prayer is more a moment-by-moment attitude than a momentary act.

OBJECTIVES

Participants will
- discover how prayer as an attitude leads to prayer as an act,
- recognize obstacles to the attitude and the act of prayer, and
- identify practical ways to make prayer part of their lifestyle.

BIBLE BASIS

Look up the Scriptures for this lesson. Then read the following background paragraphs to see how the passages relate to people today.

ROMANS 8:26-27

One obstacle that prevents many people from praying as freely as they want or should is not knowing what to say. Fortunately, as Christians we have the Holy Spirit living within us (Romans 8:9), and he conveys our innermost needs and desires to God even when we're unable to articulate them.

Just as creation "longs" for renewal (Romans 8:22), Christians "long" to be made whole, to experience life as God intended it to the fullest extent (8:23). However, sometimes we're unable to express those longings. In our moment of weakness, the Holy Spirit comes to our aid and conveys those "inexpressible longings" to God (8:26). In short, the Holy Spirit takes up our longings, makes them his own, and directs them toward God.

God, for his part, earnestly desires to know our every

thought and emotion. He's constantly searching our hearts to uncover exactly what we're thinking and feeling. Even when we don't "know" what to pray (8:26), God understands, for he "knows" the mind and the intent of the Holy Spirit, who conveys our inexpressible longings to him on our behalf (8:27). As a result of the Holy Spirit's presence within us and intercession for us, we can enjoy unending and unrestricted communication and communion with God.

EPHESIANS 6:18

God has given us the Holy Spirit to help us when we don't know what to say, but he still expects us to pray as often and as honestly as we can. Paul emphasizes that fact by repeating *pas*—the Greek word for "all" or "every"—four times in this verse. Using *every* kind of prayer and petition, we are to pray at *every* opportunity and with *all* perseverance as we petition God on behalf of *all* his people.

We can draw at least two conclusions from Paul's commands. First, we are to pray in every situation with whatever kind of prayer is appropriate to that situation. This implies that there are as many kinds of prayers as there are situations that require prayer. One prayer may not fit all occasions, but there is a prayer for every occasion. Second, it is our responsibility to keep alert and to persevere in prayer for all Christians (including ourselves). The Holy Spirit helps us pray, but we must engage ourselves in and commit ourselves to prayer at all times.

Paul also instructs us to pray "in the Spirit." Scholars explain this phrase in different ways—as referring to a prayer language, to prayer as a mystical experience, or to praying in communion with the Spirit—but it seems best to understand it as a general statement concerning our reliance on the Holy Spirit's leading and enabling in prayer (see Ephesians 2:22; 3:5; and 5:18 for the same Greek phrase). At the very least, we should open ourselves to and respond to the Holy Spirit's influence on us as we pray. In addition, we should recognize that we are as reliant on God's Spirit when we know what to pray as when we don't know what to say.

1 THESSALONIANS 5:17

Paul's two-word command to "pray continually" appears simple and straightforward until one tries to obey what it literally says. Because it's impossible always to be engaged in the act of prayer, some scholars have suggested that Paul means for Christians to pray on all occasions or to make prayer a regular part of their spiritual lives. However, the wording of this command differs from that of Ephesians 6:18, where Paul teaches that we are to pray at every opportunity. This command is also different from those around it, namely, the instructions to be joyful "at all times" and to give thanks "in all circumstances" (1 Thessalonians 5:16, 18).

Therefore, Paul probably has something other than the *act* of prayer in view here. Prayer is also an *attitude* of openness to God, an awareness of his constant presence, and the enjoyment of unending fellowship with him. In all likelihood, Paul's focus here is on prayer as an attitude, not on prayer as an act. Paul wants us to remain constantly open to and aware of God's presence with us. As we continually maintain this attitude, we will regularly express it in the act of prayer.

Most Christians would like prayer to play a more important role in their lives than it currently does. Unfortunately, even dedicated Christians struggle to pray as honestly and as often as they'd like. They don't understand that prayer is more an attitude of openness to God and his presence than a formal act that they have to perform. Use this lesson to teach your class members how to practice the true nature of prayer as an ongoing attitude.

THIS LESSON AT A GLANCE

Section	Minutes	What Participants Will Do	Supplies
OPENING	*up to 10*	**PICTURES OF PRAYER**—Discuss what their prayer lives look like and what they'd like them to look like.	"Pictures of Prayer" handouts (p. 25)
BIBLE EXPLORATION AND APPLICATION	*25 to 35*	☐ *Option 1:* **NATURAL ACTS**—Discover why prayer feels unnatural, then learn from Ephesians 6:18 and 1 Thessalonians 5:17 how to make prayer natural and continual.	Bibles, marker, newsprint, paper, pencils
	30 to 40	☐ *Option 2:* **ACTIVE ATTITUDES**—Compare prayer and love, then discover from Romans 8:26-27 and Ephesians 6:18 how to practice prayer as an attitude and as an act.	Bibles, marker, newsprint
CLOSING	*up to 10*	**THE CLOSING ACT**—Evaluate how well the class maintained the attitude of prayer, then pray for each other.	
FOR EXTRA TIME	*up to 10*	**PRAYER INVENTORY**—Discuss when they pray and what this reveals about their views of prayer.	
	up to 10	**TIME TO PRAY**—Pray silently and discuss how a regular silent-prayer time might promote a constant attitude of prayer.	

To emphasize that prayer is more an attitude than an act, the body of the lesson does not provide for a special time of individual or group prayer. At the end of the lesson, you'll be directed to call attention to that fact and to discuss how we can practice prayer as an attitude no matter what is going on around us.

THE POINT▷

OPENING

Pictures of Prayer
(up to 10 minutes)

Before class, make one photocopy of the "Pictures of Prayer" handout (p. 25) for every four class members.

Say: **Welcome to the first week of our course on prayer. During the next four weeks, we'll explore issues such as how to make prayer a constant part of our daily lives, how God answers our prayers, and how to pray when life is bad as well as when it's good. Today we'll begin by examining the idea that ▷ prayer is more a moment-by-moment attitude than a momentary act.**

Instruct people to form groups of four. Give each group a copy of the "Pictures of Prayer" handout and have group members follow the instructions at the top of the handout.

After five minutes, ask people to report which pictures they selected. Ask for volunteers to report why they chose their pictures. Then have group members discuss the following questions. Ask:

● **What do you like most about your prayer life?**

● **What about it would you like to change or improve?**

● **Which picture would you like your prayer life to be like?**

● **What appeals to you most about that depiction of prayer?**

Say: **Even if your prayer life resembles the picture you prefer, there are probably things about it that you'd like to improve. At the very least, we all can make prayer a more vital and constant part of our daily experiences. Today we'll learn how a clear understanding of the nature of prayer frees us to experience and to enjoy the constant presence of God in prayer.**

BIBLE EXPLORATION AND APPLICATION

☐ OPTION 1:
Natural Acts
(25 to 35 minutes)

Form pairs and have partners sit or stand facing each other. Instruct partners to look at each other without speaking until you tell them it's time to stop.

Allow partners to look at each other for at least one minute, then call time. Direct each pair to join another pair to form a group of four. Have group members discuss the following questions. After each question, ask for volunteers to report their groups' responses to the rest of the class. Ask:

- **What emotions did silently staring at your partner evoke?**

- **How comfortable was it for you to stare at your partner?**

- **What might make it easier for you to stare at your partner?**

- **How is this experience like your experience with prayer? How is it different?**

Say: **Sometimes prayer feels as uncomfortable as staring at someone without talking. Of course, the more uncomfortable we feel doing something, including praying, the less likely we are to actually do it. However, God never intended prayer to be an uncomfortable or unpleasant chore. He wants prayer to be as natural as the beating of our hearts.**

Instruct groups to read **Ephesians 6:18** and **1 Thessalonians 5:17.** While groups are reading, write the following questions on a sheet of newsprint and hang it where everyone can see it:

- What processes does your body perform continually? regularly?

- How might these processes be like praying continually? regularly?

- How is praying continually different from praying regularly?

- What do these passages imply about prayer as an attitude? as an act?

Have group members discuss the questions. After about eight minutes, ask for volunteers to report their groups' responses to the questions. Then say: **Since prayer is to be as comfortable and as constant as breathing, we need to make it ▶ more a moment-by-moment attitude than a momentary act. Let's see what we can do to help each other make prayer a more comfortable part of our lives.**

Have the entire class call out reasons that prayer sometimes feels unnatural or uncomfortable, reasons such as a sense of distance from God, not knowing what words to use, or feelings that prayer must be formal. Hang a sheet of newsprint where everyone can see it and write the reasons on the newsprint, leaving space to write below or

◀ **THE POINT**

If possible, give each group no more than two reasons. It's OK if several groups discuss the same reason.

beside each reason.

After you have seven or eight reasons listed, divide the reasons among the groups. Then have group members brainstorm two practical ideas for overcoming each obstacle to comfortable prayer. For example, one could suggest that people who think prayer must be formal should imagine that God is a best friend and talk to him as such. Give each group a sheet of paper and a pencil to record its ideas.

After five minutes, ask groups to report their ideas. Record the ideas on the newsprint. Give the entire class the opportunity to add any other suggestions that might be helpful. Then have people each answer the following questions within their groups. Ask:

● **Which of the reasons listed makes prayer unnatural for you?**

● **How can you overcome that obstacle to prayer next week?**

THE POINT ▷

Say: **Praying to God should be as comfortable and as continual as spending time with and talking to our closest friend. Since ▶ prayer is more a moment-by-moment attitude than a momentary act, we should remind ourselves of God's presence with us every moment of every day. When we do, we'll discover that the act of prayer becomes as natural and as constant as the beating of our hearts.**

■■■■■■■■■■■■■■■■■■■■■■■■■■■■■■■

FOR *Even Deeper*
DISCUSSION

Form groups of four or fewer to discuss the following questions:

● What does it mean to pray "in the Spirit"? Does praying in the Spirit involve our minds? our hearts? both?

● What role does listening to God play in prayer? How can we tell when God is talking to us? How can we know when it's not God?

■■■■■■■■■■■■■■■■■■■■■■■■■■■■■■■

□ **OPTION 2:**
Active Attitudes
(30 to 40 minutes)

Keep people in their groups of four. Have people each think of one person they love deeply and tell their group members about that person. After several minutes, instruct group members to discuss the following questions. After each question, ask for volunteers to report their groups' responses to the rest of the class. Ask:

- Without using the word "love," how would you describe your attitude toward your loved one?

- How is your loving attitude toward that person reflected in your actions?

- To what extent does your love continue when you're not doing anything to show it? when you're asleep?

- What is the proper relationship between the attitude of love and acts of love?

Say: **Just as love is both an attitude and actions, true prayer involves both an attitude and actions.**

Instruct group members to discuss the following questions. After each question, ask for volunteers to summarize their groups' responses for the rest of the class. Ask:

- Without using the word "pray," how would you describe the attitude of prayer?

- How should the attitude of prayer be reflected in our actions?

- To what extent can we maintain an attitude of prayer when we're not praying? when we're asleep?

- What is the proper relationship between prayer as an attitude and prayer as an act?

Say: **As we discovered in the opening, probably everyone would like his or her prayer life to be better in some way. In many cases, we'd like to enjoy** ▶ **prayer as a moment-by-moment attitude and not merely as a momentary act. Fortunately, God has given us a number of resources to help us experience the attitude and the act of prayer as we'd like.**

Have group members read and discuss **Ephesians 6:18** and **Romans 8:26-27.** Ask half the groups to identify what God has given us to make prayer as attitude easier and half to identify what God has given us to make prayer as an act easier. Encourage groups to use other biblical passages (if time permits) to supplement their lists.

Allow groups five minutes to read and discuss the passages, then ask for a volunteer from each group to report one of the group's discoveries. Begin with groups identifying what God has given us to make prayer as an attitude easier. Hang a sheet of newsprint where everyone can see it, and record groups' answers on the newsprint. Have groups continue reporting until every group has reported and every God-given resource that groups discovered has been listed.

Then say: **Think back to the image of prayer you selected in the opening.** (Pause.) **Now discuss the following questions with your group members.** Ask:

TEACHER
TIP

If people have difficulty describing prayer as an attitude, use what you learned in the Bible Basis to spur their thinking in the right direction.

◀ T H E   P O I N T

BIBLE
I N S I G H T

According to Romans 8:26-27 and Ephesians 6:18, God enables us to maintain an attitude of prayer by having the Holy Spirit live within us, by assuring us that the Holy Spirit conveys our longings to God, and by encouraging us to rely on the Holy Spirit's leading and empowering in prayer. God helps us practice the act of prayer by providing various kinds of prayers and by telling us what we should be praying for.

- What is the greatest obstacle keeping you from experiencing prayer as you'd like?

- What has God given you to help you experience the attitude of prayer that you'd like? the acts of prayer that you'd like?

- How can God's resources help you overcome your obstacle to a meaningful prayer life?

- What one thing will you do this week to appropriate God's resources for your prayer life?

Say: **Prayer is most meaningful when it arises from a moment-by-moment awareness of and openness to God's presence with us. As you go about your business during the coming week, remind yourself of all that God has done to help you practice prayer as an ongoing attitude. As you do, you'll discover that the act of prayer will begin to feel as natural as a casual conversation with your closest friend.**

■ ■

FOR *Even Deeper* DISCUSSION

Form groups of four or fewer to discuss the following questions:

- To what extent should we engage in the act of prayer when we don't have a prayerful attitude? What should we say to God when we don't feel like praying?

- To what extent can we be completely honest with God about what we're thinking or feeling? Is there anything we cannot say to God? If so, what might it be? How should we deal with thoughts and feelings that aren't complimentary to God?

■ ■

Apply·It·To·Life™ *This Week!*

The "Apply-It-To-Life This Week!" handout (p. 26) helps people further explore the issues uncovered in today's class. Give everyone a photocopy of the handout. Encourage class members to take time during the coming week to explore the questions and activities on the handout.

The Closing Act

(up to 10 minutes)

Keep people in their groups from the previous activity. Say: **You may have noticed that we haven't engaged in the act of prayer during this class. But since** **prayer is more a moment-by-moment attitude than a momentary act, we may have been praying anyway.**

Ask the entire class the following questions:

 ◁ **T H E   P O I N T**

- **How do you think we maintained an attitude of prayer during class?**

- **How could we have made prayer a more important part of our class?**

- **How can we make prayer a vital part of our lives during the week?**

Have group members close by praying for each other, asking God to help them practice prayer as a continual attitude and as a frequent act. Encourage people to allow each person to pray in the manner in which he or she is most comfortable, whether that be silently or aloud.

For Extra Time

PRAYER INVENTORY

(up to 10 minutes)

Form groups of four. Have group members discuss the following questions regarding when and where people should pray. Ask:

- **How important is it to pray before dinner? before eating a snack?**

- **How important is it to pray before a long trip? before going to the store?**

- **How important is it to pray during church services? during TV commercials?**

Ask for volunteers to report their groups' responses. Then ask the entire class the following questions. Ask:

- **What do our responses reveal about our view of prayer?**

- **How can we pray even during the normal times of the day?**

TIME TO PRAY

(up to 10 minutes)

Tell people to spend five minutes in silent communion with God, telling him exactly what they think and feel, and listening to whatever he might say to them. Encourage people each to find a quiet spot that will enable them to focus entirely on God and his presence with them.

After five minutes, call people back and ask the entire class the following questions:

- **How did spending time silently with God promote an attitude of prayer?**

- **How can you practice a regular time of silent communion with God?**

- **How might this regular time help you maintain an attitude of prayer?**

Pictures of Prayer

Have everyone in the group take turns answering the questions below. After five minutes, you'll report your answers to the rest of the class.

- Which picture best portrays your experiences with prayer?
- In what ways does this picture represent your prayer life?

Apply·It·To·Life™
This Week!

Straight From the Heart

Prayer is more a moment-by-moment attitude than a momentary act.

**Romans 8:26-27;
Ephesians 6:18; and
1 Thessalonians 5:17**

Reflecting on God's Word

Each day this week, read one of the following Scriptures and examine what it teaches about prayer as a lifestyle. Then consider how you can apply the message of the passage to your life. List your discoveries in the space under each passage.

Day 1: Isaiah 29:13-14. Real prayer begins with the heart, not with the mouth.

Day 2: Philippians 4:6-7. Telling God our requests enables us to enjoy God's peace.

Day 3: Psalm 63:1-4. Prayer arises from our longing to spend time with God.

Day 4: Luke 6:12-13. Jesus prayed all night long before making a big decision.

Day 5: Psalm 55:16-19. We can pray to God at any time about any problem.

Day 6: Luke 11:5-13. We should persistently ask God to give us what we need.

Beyond Reflection

In Deuteronomy 6:4-9, Moses instructed the Israelites to wear physical objects that would remind them of God's commands at all times. You can apply the same principle to help you maintain the constant attitude of prayer. Make or buy an object such as a small heart (to represent that prayer should be as constant as a heartbeat) and wear the object as often as you can. You may also use an object you already wear at all times—for example, a ring or a watch—to remind you of God's constant presence with you and to promote your continual communion with him.

Coming Next Week: The Right Answer Every Time
(Matthew 7:7-11 and 2 Corinthians 12:1-10)

The Right Answer Every Time

God answers each prayer with wisdom and love.

◀ THE POINT

OBJECTIVES

Participants will
- discover how and why God answers their requests as he does,
- discuss how God has answered their prayers in the past, and
- learn how they are to pray with persistence and acceptance.

BIBLE BASIS

Look up the Scriptures for this lesson. Then read the following background paragraphs to see how the passages relate to people today.

MATTHEW 7:7-11

People who doubt that their prayers really make a difference do not, as a rule, pray as persistently or as confidently as they could. In this passage, however, Jesus provides a compelling reason for his followers always to ask God for what they want and need. He assures us that persistent prayer always generates positive results.

In verses 7-8, Jesus promises that those who persist in prayer will receive what they ask for. Although it is tempting to question such a bold statement, Jesus' words are clear. First, Jesus is talking about prayer, for the three terms he uses—ask, seek, knock—refer to prayer in other biblical passages as well as in extrabiblical texts. Second, the need for persistence in prayer is conveyed by the use of the present tense of the verbs in the Greek text of these verses. Translated literally, Jesus commands his followers to "continue asking/seeking/knocking" because "everyone asking/seeking/knocking" receives his or her request. Finally, Luke confirms this understanding of Jesus' words by prefacing his version of the promise (Luke 11:9-13) with a parable teaching that those who persist in prayer will get what they ask for (Luke 11:5-8).

However, this doesn't mean that God must answer our requests just as we make them. Matthew 7:9-11 interprets the promise of the prior verses and explains in greater detail what we can expect to receive. By arguing from the lesser parent–child relationship to the greater divine–human relationship, Jesus concludes that God always gives us what is good for us. Just as parents give good gifts to their children, God answers his children's requests in ways that benefit them. Children who ask their parents for bread do not receive stones—nor, presumably, moldy bread nor even good bread if it would be harmful to them. In the same way, we as God's children can be certain we will receive only good things from him. Therefore, we can pray persistently for what we want and trust God to give us the good things we ask for and actually need.

2 CORINTHIANS 12:1-10

According to this passage, God may deny our request for a good thing when there is a greater good he wants us to have instead. Although Paul did not set out specifically to teach this principle in this text, its truth becomes clear as we read about how God responded to Paul's request to be delivered from a humiliating affliction.

Paul's primary purpose in 2 Corinthians 10–13 was to answer the accusations and attacks of some teachers at Corinth who were claiming an apostolic status superior to his. Paul defended himself mostly by "boasting" in the things that showed his "weaknesses" (see 11:30). To that end, Paul described in 12:1-10 an extraordinary experience that could have been the source of great pride (as well as a clear demonstration of his superiority) but that actually showed how God's power was most evident in Paul's weakness.

Biblical scholars have explained Paul's "thorn in the flesh" in a number of ways, including persecution, unfulfilled sexual desires, epilepsy, bad vision, a speech impediment, or some other physical malady. Had Paul thought it important for us to know the precise nature of his affliction, he would have told us. As it is, Paul intends us to learn from God's refusal to lift his torment that God's strength is magnified in our weaknesses.

When Paul was "caught up" to the third heaven in a vision or in his spirit, he heard things too awful and amazing for any human to repeat. This experience could have made Paul proud of himself, so God allowed Paul to be humbled by some unknown affliction that Paul regarded as "a messenger of Satan" (verse 7). On three different occasions Paul asked God to remove his torment. God, however, denied each request, explaining that Paul's weakness was vital to the demonstration of Christ's power in his life and ministry. Paul, for his part, accepted God's answer and even "considered it good" (Greek: *eudokeō*—verse 10). Like Paul, we can persistently ask for what we want, for what we think is good for us. However, we should also follow Paul's example of accepting God's clear denial of our requests as a sign of his wise and loving care for us.

None of us likes to be told no, even when we know that it might be for our own good. But saying no is part of every relationship, including that with our loving God. Use this lesson to teach people how God answers every request we make (including those he denies) with the wisdom and the love that only he possesses.

THIS LESSON AT A GLANCE

Section	Minutes	What Participants Will Do	Supplies
OPENING	up to 10	**JUST SAY NO**—Compare telling other people yes and no to God's answers to their prayers.	
BIBLE EXPLORATION AND APPLICATION	25 to 35	☐ Option 1: **LEARNING TO TRUST**—Experience giving and receiving good things, then learn from Matthew 7:7-11 how God always gives them good things.	Bibles, glass of vinegar, vase of flowers, fruit plate, mousetrap, blindfolds, newsprint, marker
	30 to 40	☐ Option 2: **REASONABLE ANSWERS**—Help each other navigate an obstacle course and discover from Matthew 7:7-11 and 2 Corinthians 12:1-10 how and why God answers our prayers as he does.	Bibles, blindfolds, "Reasonable Answers" handouts (p. 37), pencils
CLOSING	up to 10	**PRAYER CONNECTIONS**—Use yarn to show how they link themselves to God and to each other through prayer.	Skein of yarn for every 10 class members, scissors
⏱ **FOR EXTRA TIME**	up to 10	**MORE REASONS**—Study various biblical passages to discover additional reasons God answers prayer as he does.	Bibles, "Apply-It-To-Life This Week!" handouts (p. 38), pencils
	up to 10	**PARENTAL RESPONSES**—Compare how they would answer a child's request to how God answers their requests.	

Just Say No

(up to 10 minutes)

Say: **Last week we discovered that prayer is more a moment-by-moment attitude than a momentary act. However,** sometimes even our sincerest requests aren't answered as we'd like. That shouldn't surprise us, however, because it's the same way in our relationships with each other.

Have people form pairs. Ask partners to take turns describing a time they told someone no even though it hurt that person's feelings. After several minutes, have partners take turns describing a time they told someone yes against their better judgment. After several minutes, ask the entire class the following questions:

● **How did you feel when you told the person no? when you told the person yes?**

● **What resulted from saying no to that person? from saying yes to that person?**

● **How are these answers like God's answers to prayer? How are they different?**

Say: **It's often difficult to tell someone no, even when we know it's for the best. It's also hard to be told no, even when the one telling us no is God. But it's a little easier to accept disappointing answers when we recognize that ▷ God answers each prayer with wisdom and love.**

T H E   **P** O I N T ▷

BIBLE **E**XPLORATION **AND A**PPLICATION

☐ **O**PTION **1:**

Learning to Trust

(25 to 35 minutes)

Before class, prepare the following items: a drinking glass full of vinegar, a vase of flowers, a mousetrap, and a plate full of fruit pieces. Keep these items out of sight until you are directed to bring them out later in the activity.

Keep people in their pairs from the opening activity. Have each pair choose one partner to be blindfolded. Pass out the blindfolds and instruct the seeing partners to blindfold their partners.

After all the blindfolds are on, set out the items you prepared before class. Set the mousetrap. Then call the seeing partners aside and instruct them to give their partners what they request unless it is something that would be distasteful or harmful. Specifically, seeing partners should give fruit to anyone who asks for the drink or the food and a flower to anyone who asks for the item to touch or the item to smell.

Instruct the seeing people to rejoin their partners. Say: **I've set out four items: something to eat, something to drink, something to touch, and something to smell. Those of you who are blindfolded need to decide which of the four you'd like and then ask your partner to bring you that item. Your partner has been instructed to respond to your request.**

After everyone has been served, have blindfolded partners remove their blindfolds. Show them the four items and give them the chance to exchange what they were given for what they requested. Pass around the plate of fruit so everyone can have a snack. Then ask the entire class the following questions:

- **Blindfolded partners, how do you feel about your partner's response to your request?**

- **Seeing partners, what was it like to be able to override your partner's instructions?**

- **How is this activity like how God responds to our requests? How is it different?**

Say: **God hears everything we say, including our praise and our petitions, but he doesn't always respond to our prayers in the way we want or expect. In 2 Corinthians 12, for example, we read that Paul asked God to take away a troubling "thorn in the flesh" but that God didn't.** Read **2 Corinthians 12:6-10.** Say: **Another portion of God's Word helps us understand why God said no to Paul and why he sometimes says no to our requests.**

Have each pair join another pair to form a group of four. Direct the groups to read **Matthew 7:7-11.** While groups are reading, write the following questions on a sheet of newsprint and hang it where everyone can see it. Write:
- What is our responsibility when we pray?
- What is God's responsibility when we pray?
- How will God respond to each of our prayers?

After about five minutes, ask for volunteers to report their groups' answers to the rest of the class. Say: **Even when God doesn't give us what we want or expect, we can trust ▷ God to respond to each of our prayers with wisdom and love. Let's talk about how that wisdom and goodness might be evident even in a difficult situation.**

Have group members briefly discuss the following situa-

TEACHER TIP

It's unlikely anyone will exchange the good thing they received for the bad thing they requested. However, if someone does, use this teachable moment to talk about why we sometimes refuse the good things God gives us and hurt ourselves by holding on to things that are bad for us.

◁ **THE POINT**

tion. Say: **Suppose someone you know becomes ill and dies even though you and many other Christians prayed for healing. In what specific ways might God's answer to those prayers be considered wise and loving?**

After approximately five minutes, ask people to report what their groups concluded. Then have each person silently answer the following questions. Pause one minute after each question. Ask:

- **What is one request that you have made or would like to make to God?**

- **How might God show his wisdom and love by granting your request? by denying it? by making you wait? by giving you something else?**

THE POINT

Say: **Although we can't know how God will answer our requests, we can be certain that ▶ God will answer each prayer with wisdom and love. That should encourage us to continue asking God for what we need and to trust God when he answers our prayers in ways we might not want or expect.**

■■■■■■■■■■■■■■■■■■■■■■■■■■■

FOR *Even Deeper* **DISCUSSION**

Form groups of four or fewer to discuss the following questions:

- Read Isaiah 59:2-3 and Jeremiah 14:11-12. To what extent does God always hear our praise? our requests? To what extent does God always accept our praise? our requests?

- What must we do for God to hear and accept our praise? to hear and grant our requests? What kinds of things might cause God to reject our praise? our requests?

■■■■■■■■■■■■■■■■■■■■■■■■■■■

□ **OPTION 2:**
Reasonable Answers
(30 to 40 minutes)

Before class, make one photocopy of the "Reasonable Answers" handout (p. 37) for each class member.

Have people remain in their pairs. (If you completed Option 1, have people re-form the pairs from the opening activity.) Have each pair choose one partner to be blindfolded and one to be a leader. Pass out the blindfolds and instruct the leaders to blindfold their partners.

After all the blindfolds are on, arrange the chairs in your classroom to create an obstacle course from one side

TEACHER TIP

If you completed Option 1, have partners who were blindfolded serve as the leaders in this activity.

of the room to the other (see diagram in the margin). Have the leaders guide their partners to the start of the obstacle course and help them line up across that side of the room.

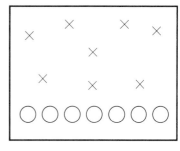

Say: **Those of you who are blindfolded have two minutes to navigate your way through the chairs we've set out to reach the other side of the room. Before you make each move, you must ask your leader for specific guidance. For example, you might ask, "Can I take two steps to the left?" or "Can I take four steps forward?" Leaders, you are to help your partners move through the obstacle course safely and quickly by answering "yes," "no," or "wait" to each request. Ready? Go.**

After two minutes, have leaders help their partners remove their blindfolds. Then ask the entire class the following questions:

- **How well did the leaders help their partners across the room? How could they have done even better?**

- **How are the answers the leaders gave like God's answers to our prayers? How are they different?**

- **Why did the leaders deny some of the requests? grant some? sometimes make their partners wait?**

Say: **Just as the leaders in this activity responded to each request to produce the greatest progress, God answers each of our requests to bring about the greatest good. And even though we don't always know why God answers our prayers as he does, God's Word helps us understand some of the reasons behind God's answers.**

Have each pair join another pair to form a foursome. Give each person a copy of the "Reasonable Answers" handout and a pencil. Assign half the groups the **Matthew 7:7-11** section of the handout and the rest of the groups the **2 Corinthians 12:1-10** section. Instruct groups to follow the instructions at the top of their sections.

After 10 minutes, have groups take turns reporting what they discovered. Encourage people to fill in the section of the handout that they didn't complete within their groups. After you have discussed both biblical passages, ask the entire class the following questions:

- **What are the different answers God can give to a request?** (Yes; no; wait; here's something else.)

- **Why might God grant a request? deny a request? make us wait for our request? give us something else?**

BIBLE INSIGHT

Since some stones resemble loaves of bread and some serpents resemble fish, giving stones and snakes for bread and fish would be deceptive (Matthew 7:9-10, compare Luke 11:11-12). The deception would also be cruel, for it would involve refusing what had been requested, deceiving the child into thinking the request had been granted, and possibly giving something harmful to the child.

TEACHER
TIP

You may want to write "yes," "no," "wait," and "here's something else" on sheets of newsprint and hang them where everyone can see them. Then you can record on the newsprint people's suggestions as to why God answers our prayers as he does.

TEACHER
TIP

If you have time, have people list a request for each of these categories: God granted the request, God denied the request, God made me wait, and God gave me something else. Then have people explain why they think God answered as he did in each case.

Say: **We don't always understand why God answers our prayers as he does, but we do know that ▶ he answers each request with wisdom and love. That's true of prayers he's answered in the past as well as of prayers we take to him today.**

Instruct everyone to list on the back of the handout an important request he or she made to God sometime in the past. Then have people write how God answered their requests and why they think God answered as he did.

After several minutes, have people re-form their original pairs and share what they've written with their partners. After both partners have reported, have them write on the back of their handouts one current request they would like God to grant. Then have partners help each other list reasons God might grant the request, deny it, make them wait for it, or answer it differently than they expect.

When both partners' requests have been discussed, have partners pray for each other's requests and for the ability to believe that God's answer will be wise and loving no matter what it is.

■■■■■■■■■■■■■■■■■■■■■■■■■■■■■■■■■

FOR *Even Deeper*
DISCUSSION

Form groups of four or fewer to discuss the following questions:

● To what extent can prayer change God's attitude toward us? God's will? another person's heart or will? the laws of nature? the one who is praying?

● How can we know when God is saying no to a request? How should we pray if we're unsure what God's answer is? Is it wrong to keep asking for something if God's not going to give it to us? if we know God's not going to give it to us?

■■■■■■■■■■■■■■■■■■■■■■■■■■■■■■■■

The "Apply-It-To-Life This Week!" handout (p. 38) helps people further explore the issues uncovered in today's class. Give everyone a photocopy of the handout. Encourage class members to take time during the coming week to explore the questions and activities on the handout.

Praeyer Connections

(up to 10 minutes)

Tell people to form a standing circle. If you have more than 10 people, form multiple circles of 10 or fewer people. Choose one person to stand in the center of the circle. Give the yarn to someone standing in the circle. (You'll need a skein of yarn or a ball of yarn at least 100 feet long for each circle.)

Say: **When we give our requests to God, he never ignores or sets them aside.** ▶**God always returns our prayers to us, answering each one with wisdom and love.**

 THE POINT

Instruct the person holding the yarn to name aloud one request he or she would like to give to God and then, while holding one end of the yarn, to toss the rest to the person in the middle of the circle. Have the center person hold on to the yarn and toss the rest back to the person who named the request. Then have that person grab the yarn once again and hand the rest to the person on his or her right. Repeat the process with everyone in the circle.

When the ball of yarn has gone around the circle and has been handed back to the first person, instruct the center person to name his or her request and then to close the group prayer by saying amen.

Say: **Prayer helps us solidify and deepen our connection to God, but it can also link us together more closely with other Christians. When you leave today, I'll give you a piece of yarn to take with you as a reminder of your prayer connection with God and with each other. Then, during the week, take all our requests to God, knowing that** ▶**he will answer each prayer with wisdom and love.**

THE POINT

Roll up the yarn, then cut off a piece for each class member. Hand each person a piece of yarn as he or she leaves the room.

⏱ For Extra Time

MORE REASONS

(up to 10 minutes)

Form three groups. (If you have more than 18 class members, divide into groups of six or fewer people.) Give everyone a copy of the "Apply-It-To-Life This Week!" handout (p. 38) and a pencil. Assign two of the biblical texts listed in the "Reflecting on God's Word" section of the handout to each group. Instruct groups to read and answer the following questions for each text:

● What does this passage teach about why God answers prayer as he does?

● How does this reveal God's wisdom and love in answering our prayers?

After five minutes, have groups report their discoveries to the rest of the class. Encourage people to take their handouts home and to reflect on the truths of all the Scriptures on the handout.

PARENTAL RESPONSES
(up to 10 minutes)

Divide the class into four groups. Tell people that they're to imagine they have an 11-year-old child who has asked them for a sandwich to eat. Then assign one of the following responses to each group:

● grant the child's request,
● deny the child's request,
● tell the child to wait, and
● give the child something else.

Instruct groups to brainstorm reasons or describe situations in which they would answer in their assigned ways.

After five minutes, ask groups to report their reasons and situations to the rest of the class. Then ask the entire class the following questions. Ask:

● **How are the reasons we listed like the reasons God answers our prayers as he does? How are they different?**

● **How should we as God's children respond to his answers to our requests? What responses should we avoid?**

Reasonable ANSWERS

☞ Matthew 7:7-11

As a group, read Matthew 7:7-11 and discuss the following questions. Take notes on the discussion—after 10 minutes you'll be given the opportunity to report your insights to the rest of the class.

➤ How does verse 11 help clarify the promise of verses 7-8?

➤ What can we be certain that God will give to us?

➤ Why might God withhold something we've requested?

➤ What must we do to receive good things from God?

☞ 2 Corinthians 12:1-10

As a group, read 2 Corinthians 12:1-10 and discuss the following questions. Take notes on the discussion—after 10 minutes you'll be given the opportunity to report your insights to the rest of the class.

➤ How can God use something bad to accomplish good?

➤ How should we respond when we experience trouble?

➤ Why might God deny our request for something good?

➤ How should we react when God turns down a request?

Apply·It·To·Life™ This Week!

The Right Answer Every Time

God answers each prayer
with wisdom and love.
**Matthew 7:7-11 and
2 Corinthians 12:1-10**

Reflecting on God's Word

Each day this week, read one of the following Scriptures and examine what it teaches about why God answers prayers as he does. Then consider how you can apply what you learn to God's answers to your prayers. List your discoveries in the space under each passage.

Day 1: 1 John 3:18-22. We receive our requests when we obey and please God.

Day 2: Matthew 26:36-44. Some requests are denied for the good of others.

Day 3: Psalm 66:16-19. God does not hear our prayers when we hold on to sin.

Day 4: Matthew 21:18-22. God answers prayers that are offered in faith.

Day 5: John 16:16-24. God gives us what we ask for in the name of Jesus.

Day 6: James 4:1-3. God grants our requests when our motives are pure.

Beyond Reflection

Starting this week, write every prayer request you have on an index card and post it in a prominent place such as on your refrigerator, above your desk, or on the mirror in your bedroom. Use the index cards to remind you to present your requests to God. Whenever God answers a prayer, write on the card how God answered the request and how that answer shows his wisdom and love for you. Then use the cards with answered prayers to remind you to thank God for his wise and loving answers to all your prayers.

Coming Next Week: Praying When Life Is Bad
(Psalms 6:1-10; 39:1-13; and 143:1-12)

Praying When Life Is Bad

We can approach God with our innermost feelings and most urgent needs.

◀ **THE POINT**

OBJECTIVES

Participants will
- discover their freedom to tell God what they think and feel,
- study biblical models for addressing complaints to God, and
- learn how to express their personal feelings and needs to God.

BIBLE BASIS

Look up the Scriptures for this lesson. Then read the following background paragraphs to see how the passages relate to people today.

Complaint psalms (also called laments or petitionary prayers) such as Psalms 6, 39, and 143 seek to accomplish two things: to inform God that something in the psalmist's life is seriously wrong and to convince God that he should make things right. As part of God's Word, complaint psalms also show us how to talk honestly to God when life becomes intolerable.

Psalm 6 models the attitude and act of biblical complaining to God in several ways. First, the psalmist calls God by name five times (Hebrew Yahweh, translated "LORD") and addresses God directly as "you" another five times in the first five verses. Biblical complaint helps us enter into conversation with God instead of silently distancing ourselves from God.

PSALM 6:1-10

INSIGHT

Psalm 6:5, like most of the Old Testament, was written before God fully revealed the concepts of resurrection, heaven, and hell. Consequently, this verse still reflects a belief in Sheol (NIV: "the grave"), which was understood to be a shadowy underworld where all people, whether good or evil, went when they died. People in Sheol did not suffer, but they were cut off from God and the joy of life in his presence. Therefore, they were unable to praise God for the present experience of his goodness to them.

PSALM 39:1-13

PSALM 143:1-12

Second, the complaint boldly requests specific changes. God is asked to replace angry discipline with divine mercy (verses 1-2a) and to deliver the psalmist from sickness and death (verses 2b, 4-5). Contrary to what we might expect, the requests are more demands than appeals. The psalmist directs God with imperative verbs not to do certain things (verse 1) and to do others (verses 2, 4).

Finally, the complaint can boldly demand change because the requests are supported by important considerations. The psalmist's condition (verses 2-3, 6-7) should elicit mercy from God and prompt him to act according to his character (verse 4b). God likewise has an interest in granting the requests. He will be deprived of praise if he allows the psalmist to die (verse 5). Therefore, it is in everyone's best interests for God to hear, accept, and answer the psalmist's complaint and petition for healing.

In general, people tend to tell others their grievances more readily than they express them to God. However, this inclination runs counter to a basic assumption of the biblical complaint psalms, namely, that when we feel compelled to speak out we should speak first and foremost to God. Psalm 39 provides a concrete example of this perspective, for in it the psalmist maintains silence before others (verses 1-3a) but speaks openly to God (verses 3b-13).

The language of the psalm is at times unflattering (verses 11, 13) and accusatory (verse 9b). However, in the midst of complaint, petition, and accusation—at the exact center of the psalm—stands an affirmation of trust in and loyalty to God (verse 7). In other words, the psalmist's complaining expresses devotion rather than defiance. We ask God to demonstrate his devotion to us as we remind him of our devotion to him. Thus, even "the accusation is a form of active hope" (Walter Brueggemann). When we complain according to the biblical pattern, we tell God how bad things have become precisely because we recognize that he alone can make them better.

The demanding and accusatory tone of the biblical complaint psalms makes some people squirm. However, the biblical writers generally provide good reasons for speaking so boldly and bluntly to God. They see an inexplicable and unacceptable inconsistency between God's character and their situation.

Psalm 143, for example, lists a number of reasons God should answer the psalmist's requests. Some concern God's character—his faithfulness (verse 1), righteousness (verses 1, 11), and loyal love (verses 8, 12)—and God's reputation (verse 11). Others reflect the severity of the psalmist's situation (verses 2-4, 7) or the depth of his loyalty to God. The psalmist, who claims to be God's servant (verses 2, 12), says "I trust you" and "You are my God" (verses 8, 10) in the same breath in which he demands an answer from God (verse 7). Because the psalmist knew and was devoted to God, he felt free to approach God boldly and to ask that he act in character on his behalf.

Like the writers of the Old Testament psalms, people today go through bad times. When they do, they need to honestly and confidently express their innermost feelings and most urgent needs to the only one who can make a difference. By following the example of the biblical psalms, your class members can become their own psalmists, composing prayers of petition (and praise) to our wise and loving God.

THIS LESSON AT A GLANCE

Section	Minutes	What Participants Will Do	Supplies
OPENING	up to 10	**PRAY ANYTHING!**—Discuss their reactions to a prayer of complaint.	
BIBLE EXPLORATION AND APPLICATION	25 to 35	☐ Option 1: **PRAYING UNDER PRESSURE**—Use balloons to measure the stress in their lives and discover from Psalms 6 and 143 how to express negative feelings to God.	Bibles, straight pins, small balloons, paper, pencils, marker, newsprint
	35 to 45	☐ Option 2: **WHEN SILENCE ISN'T GOLDEN**—Discuss how imposed silence affects relationships, then learn from Psalm 39 how to vocalize their complaints and requests to God.	Bibles, "Valid Complaints" handouts (p. 48), pencils
CLOSING	up to 5	**CONFIDENT ENOUGH TO COMPLAIN**—Remind each other of God's goodness in their lives.	
FOR EXTRA TIME	up to 10	**THROUGH OTHERS' EYES**—Write prayers of complaint from the perspective of other people.	Paper, pencils
	up to 10	**COLOR ME . . . ?**—Depict their feelings and discuss ways to clarify and communicate their emotions to God.	Markers or crayons, paper

Pray Anything!
(up to 10 minutes)

If possible, use the prayer provided in the lesson and the thoughts and ideas expressed in Psalms 10:1 and 13:1-2 as a model to write your own complaint prayer. Using a personalized prayer will be more realistic and will help people feel comfortable discussing their thoughts and emotions later on. If people feel that the prayer is inappropriate, accept their opinions and then use Psalms 10:1 and 13:1-2 to help them understand that complaint is a biblically authorized form of prayer.

THE POINT ▶

Say: **Last week we discovered that we can pray with honesty and confidence because God answers each prayer with wisdom and love. So let's begin today's class with a prayer that applies what we learned last week.**

Pray: **God, I'm really disappointed with you. Earlier this week, you disappeared on me. You let me down and left me all alone at the precise moment that I needed you most. Now I'm in real trouble, and it's your fault. So pay attention. Solve my problem; make it go away. I'm trusting you to take care of me. I'm putting myself in your loving hands. In Jesus' name, amen.**

Pause 30 seconds so people have a chance to think about your prayer, then ask the entire class the following questions:

● **What was your response to me talking to God as I did?**

● **How do you think God feels about me praying that way?**

● **How freely can we express our negative feelings to God?**

● **Why are we sometimes afraid to tell God how we feel?**

● **Why should we feel free to tell God exactly how we feel?**

Say: **When we realize that prayer is more an attitude than an act and that God answers each prayer with wisdom and love, we can tell God exactly what's on our minds and in our hearts. We feel the freedom to express every thought and every emotion. So today we're going to discuss how** ▶ **we can approach God with our innermost feelings and most urgent needs.**

☐ **OPTION 1:**
Praying Under Pressure
(25 to 35 minutes)

Give each person a balloon and a straight pin. Say: **We all go through tough times and bad situations, and often those experiences produce negative** feelings. To measure the amount of stress in your life, blow up your balloon in accordance with the following instructions. Blow into your balloon two seconds for every time . . .

- someone said something that hurt you this week.
- you've been home sick during the past six months.
- someone falsely accused you during the past month.
- a friend or family member died during the past year.
- someone questioned your motives within the last month.
- you've struggled to pay your bills during the past year.
- you fought with someone you love during the past week.
- you've felt abandoned by God during the past two years.

Finally, if you told God exactly how you felt about each of these situations, slowly let the air out of your balloon. If you didn't tell God how you felt, prick the balloon with your pin.

Then have people form groups of four to discuss the following questions. After each question, ask for volunteers to report their groups' responses to the rest of the class. Ask:

- What does this activity reveal about the amount of stress in our lives? about our success in handling stress?

- How are people who hold in negative feelings like balloons that are about to explode? How are they different?

- How can holding in negative feelings affect our relationships with others? our relationship with God? ourselves?

- How can honestly telling God exactly what's on our hearts and minds help us deal with our negative feelings?

Say: Sometimes we harm ourselves by suppressing thoughts and feelings that we should be expressing to God. The Old Testament complaint psalms, however, teach us a better way. They show us the biblical way ▶ to approach God with our innermost feelings and most urgent needs.

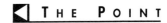 **◀ THE POINT**

Assign half the groups **Psalm 6:1-10** and half **Psalm 143:1-12.** Give each group a sheet of paper and a pencil. Instruct groups to read their assigned passages and to list the following elements of the psalms:

- specific complaints to God,
- specific requests of God, and
- reasons for confidence in God.

While groups are working, write "complaint," "request," and "confidence" on separate sheets of newsprint, and hang them where everyone can see them.

After six minutes, tell groups they have two minutes to finish their discussions. When time is up, ask groups to report what they listed for each category. Record their observations on the newsprint. Then instruct group members to discuss the following questions. After each question, ask for volunteers to report their responses to the rest of the class. Ask:

- **What do these psalms teach about our freedom to complain to God about life? about others? about God?**

- **What do they teach about how we should take our complaints and our requests to God?**

- **What's the proper relationship between complaining to God and having faith in God?**

- **How can honestly expressing our complaints to God lead to honest praise of God?**

Instruct group members each to describe one situation they would like to complain to God about and to state what they want God to do in the situation. Have people refer to the newsprint for help expressing their complaints and requests. After everyone has shared a situation, have group members pray, asking God to answer the requests that have been shared and expressing their confidence in God's good answers to their prayers.

When groups finish praying, encourage class members to keep their balloons as a reminder to express their complaints and requests to their faithful God.

■ ■

FOR *Even Deeper*
DISCUSSION

Form groups of four or fewer to discuss the following questions:

- Read Psalms 7:6 and 10:15. To what extent can we ask God to punish our enemies while obeying Jesus' command to love them (Matthew 5:44-45)? How might turning our desire for revenge over to God help us love our enemies?

- Are there thoughts or feelings we must never express to God? If so, what are they? How should we deal with negative thoughts and feelings about God?

■ ■

☐ O P T I O N 2 :
When Silence Isn't Golden
(35 to 45 minutes)

Before class, make one photocopy of the "Valid Complaints" handout (p. 48) for each class member.

Form groups of four. Instruct group members each to describe a time they were angry with someone and didn't express it to that person.

After everyone has had a chance to share, have group members discuss the following questions. Ask for volunteers to report their groups' answers after each question. Ask:

- **How did hiding your anger affect your relationship with that person? affect you?**

- **Why were you unable or unwilling to express your anger to that person?**

- **Why are we sometimes unable or unwilling to talk to God when we're angry?**

- **How does hiding your anger from God affect your relationship with him?**

Say: **Because God already knows everything about us, ▷ we can confidently approach him with our innermost feelings and most urgent needs. In fact, Psalm 39 shows us how to pray when we're angry and want God to do something about it.**

Give each person a copy of the "Valid Complaints" handout and a pencil. Tell group members to follow the instructions to complete the top half of the handout.

After 10 minutes, ask for volunteers to report their groups' discoveries. Then ask the entire class the following questions:

- **What does this psalm teach about when to be silent? when to speak up?**

- **Why can we honestly tell God how we feel? what we want him to do?**

- **How does telling God our innermost feelings and most urgent needs help us? our relationship with him?**

- **How will God respond to our innermost feelings? answer our urgent requests?**

Then direct people to follow the instructions to complete the bottom half of the "Valid Complaints" handout.

After five minutes, have people silently pray what they wrote on the handout. When people finish praying, invite group members to share what they wrote with each other. Then instruct group members to pray together, asking

◀ **THE POINT**

God to answer the requests that have been shared and expressing their confidence that God will answer their requests in the best way possible.

■ ■

FOR *Even Deeper* **DISCUSSION**

Form groups of four or fewer to discuss the following questions:

● When it is necessary to be silent before God? to speak to God? What are the dangers of always telling God what we're thinking and feeling? of never telling God?

● To what extent must we be careful about what we ask God to do? Will God give us things that go against his will? that harm us? If so, when and why might God do this?

■ ■

Apply·It·To·Life™
This Week!

The "Apply-It-To-Life This Week!" handout (p. 49) helps people further explore the issues uncovered in today's class. Give everyone a photocopy of the handout. Encourage class members to take time during the coming week to explore the questions and activities on the handout.

TEACHER TIP

If you have more than 15 people in your class, form multiple circles of 15 or fewer.

CLOSING

Confident Enough to Complain

(up to 5 minutes)

Have people form a standing circle. Read **Psalm 143:5-6,** then say: **The writers of the Old Testament psalms often recounted and remembered God's goodness in the past to help themselves remain confident in the midst of their current troubles. Reminding ourselves of good things God has done also prepares us to face any problems that might come our way tomorrow.**

Invite people to take turns naming aloud an answered prayer or some other evidence of God's goodness in their lives.

When everyone who wants to has shared, say: **When life is bad, it's hard to remember that God is good. But God is always good, and he always answers our prayers with wisdom and love, even when he doesn't give us what we've asked for. So next time your life seems bad, remember God's faithfulness and good-**

ness to your classmates and to yourself.

Ask people to join hands, then close in prayer, thanking God for the freedom  to confidently approach him with our innermost feelings and most urgent needs.

 For Extra Time

THROUGH OTHERS' EYES

(up to 10 minutes)

Form groups of four. Give each group a sheet of paper and a pencil. Assign each group one of the following situations:

- You are an Ethiopian woman whose child is starving.
- You are a father of four who has cancer.
- You are single mother of two who's just lost her job.
- You are a student who's been falsely accused of cheating.
- You are an unemployed teacher who's lost his home.

Instruct groups to write complaint prayers that include a realistic complaint about the situation, specific requests to God, and expressions of confidence in God's goodness.

After five minutes, have groups read their complaint prayers to the rest of the class. Then ask the entire class the following questions:

- **How are the complaints we have like these complaints? How are they different?**

- **How can reminding ourselves of others' needs help us put our own in perspective?**

COLOR ME...?

(up to 10 minutes)

Set out a number of different colored markers or crayons. Give everyone a sheet of paper. Instruct people to use the markers or crayons to draw symbolic representations of their deepest feelings. For example, someone who is angry might draw a red picture, while someone else might use gray to depict feelings of gloominess.

After several minutes, have people form small groups made up as much as possible of people who used the same colors. Tell group members to explain their pictures to one another and to help each other list adjectives that describe or clarify their feelings. Then have group members discuss the following questions:

- **How can depicting our feelings help us clarify them? tell God about them?**

- **What other techniques can help us clarify our feelings? convey them to God?**

VALID COMPLAINTS

Working together as a group, read Psalm 39:1-13 and discuss the following questions. Take notes on your discussion—after 10 minutes you'll be asked to report your insights to the rest of the class.

► **WHAT** is the psalmist's view of and reaction to his situation?

► **WHAT** different feelings does the psalmist have about God?

► **WHY** was the psalmist quiet before others but vocal to God?

► **WHAT** specifically does the psalmist want God to do for him?

Working on your own, apply what you learned by writing your own complaint prayer. Think of a situation in your life that you'd like God to change, then follow the instructions below to tell God how you feel and to ask for his help in that situation. After five minutes, you'll have an opportunity to share with your group members what you've written.

► **COMPLAINT:** Describe to God your view of and feelings about the situation.

► **REQUEST:** State to God what specifically you want him to do in this situation.

► **CONFIDENCE:** Tell God why you trust him to answer your prayer with wisdom and love.

Praying When Life Is Bad

We can approach God with our innermost feelings and most urgent needs.
Psalms 6:1-10; 39:1-13; and 143:1-12

Reflecting on God's Word

Each day this week, read one of the following prayers and examine how it expresses complaints and requests to God. Then consider how you can apply what you learn to your own prayer life. List your discoveries in the space under each passage.

Day 1: Psalm 10:1-18. A complaint about the prosperity of the wicked.

Day 2: Psalm 28:1-9. A request not to be judged along with evil people.

Day 3: Psalm 55:1-23. A complaint about a deceptive friend's disloyalty.

Day 4: Psalm 77:1-20. A plea for God to be gracious now as in the past.

Day 5: Psalm 88:1-18. A complaint about impending death and desertion.

Day 6: Jeremiah 20:7-18. A claim that God has mistreated the prophet.

Beyond Reflection

Set aside 10 minutes at the beginning of each day to identify your greatest need for that day. Record the need on an index card and then write underneath it reasons God should meet your need. Reasons might relate to the details of your situation, your loyalty to God, or God's character. Carry the card with you during the day as a reminder to boldly approach God with your innermost feelings and most urgent needs.

Coming Next Week: Praying When Life Is Good
(Psalms 30:1-12; 113:1-9; and James 5:13)

Praying When Life Is Good

We honor God with honest praise and open thanks.

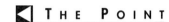 **THE POINT**

OBJECTIVES

Participants will
- discuss how praise affects God and their relationship with him,
- examine select psalms to learn biblical principles of praise, and
- discover ways to praise and thank God during their daily lives.

BIBLE BASIS

Look up the Scriptures for this lesson. Then read the following background paragraphs to see how the passages relate to people today.

Behind James' command to pray during good and bad times lies an important biblical principle, that there is a prayer appropriate to every situation. We can talk freely to God regardless of our physical circumstances or our emotional state. In the midst of suffering, we can approach God honestly with our needs, and when we're cheerful, we can (and should) share our joy with God and with others.

JAMES 5:13

Thanksgiving psalms and hymns such as Psalms 30 and 113 played an important role in ancient Israelite worship. These prayers and songs guided Old Testament believers as they expressed their gratitude to and adoration of God. As part of our Bible, they also teach us important principles of praise and thanks that we can apply to our own situations today.

PSALM 30:1-12

For example, Psalm 30 models several important elements of the kind of thanks that God desires. First, biblical thanks is honest and realistic. This psalmist thanks God for answering his prayer and saving him from death (verses 2-3, 6-12), which assumes that the psalmist's life was in real danger. Biblical praise and thanks arose from an appreciation of God's ability to bring good out of evil, not from a denial of the presence of evil. In ancient Israel, thanks was a concrete reaction to a real experience rather than an abstract reflection on a hypothetical truth.

Second, biblical thanks is expressed in the presence of God (verses 1-3, 6-12) and other believers (verses 4-5). More often than not, the psalmist offering thanks would invite other worshipers to hear what God had done and to share in the festive celebration of God's tangible goodness (see Psalms 22:22, 25; 32:8-11; 34:1-3, 11-22; Leviticus 7:11-21). By offering thanks within the community of believers, the psalmist both honored God with public gratitude and encouraged others with practical guidance.

PSALM 113:1-9

Like the thanks expressed in Psalm 30, the praise declared by Psalm 113 was offered within the context of the community (verses 1-3, 9c). Authentic faith is rarely silent, so the psalmists freely and publicly voiced their pains as well as their praises, and their sufferings along with God's saving acts. In contrast to the modern tendency to privatize and to muffle one's faith commitment, this psalm invites God's people to lift their voices together in public praise of God.

Psalm 113 also teaches us to praise God both for who he is (God's character) and for what he does (God's deeds). To reveal how God's character and deeds interrelate, the psalmist describes God's exalted position (verses 4-6) and his active concern for those lacking power or social status (verses 7-9). God, who sits enthroned above every natural and supernatural power, lovingly stoops down to lift the poor and the powerless out of the dust, out of their distress. The only appropriate response to such greatness and goodness is honest and open praise.

Finally, this psalm implies that praise should involve one's entire self. In between an opening and closing call to praise (verses 1-3, 9c), the psalm provides the content of praise (verses 4-9b). The calls to praise speak to the heart; the content of praise speaks to the mind. Consequently, when we praise we should neither empty our minds and simply emote nor merely repeat pious words devoid of emotion and personal significance. Genuine praise requires us to lift our hearts in honest devotion to and our minds in full engagement with our good and loving God.

Most Christians know they should praise and thank God more regularly and genuinely than they do. However, all too many really don't know how to freely express their honest praise and open thanks to God. Use this lesson to help your class members discover natural and creative ways to honor God with sincere appreciation for his kind and caring presence in their lives.

THIS LESSON AT A GLANCE

Section	Minutes	What Participants Will Do	Supplies
OPENING	up to 10	**THE POWER OF PRAISE**—Discuss how praise and thanks affects them and how their praise and thanks affects God.	Bible
BIBLE EXPLORATION AND APPLICATION	25 to 35	☐ Option 1: **THE RIGHT INGREDIENTS**—Compare refreshments lacking ingredients to deficient praise and discuss Psalm 30 to identify the ingredients of praise.	Bibles, cookies, pitchers of soft drink mix, cups, napkins, marker, newsprint
	30 to 40	☐ Option 2: **PERSONALIZING PRAISE**—Praise God, then compare their expressions of praise to the model presented in Psalm 113.	Bibles, "Praise, Biblical Style" handouts (p. 61), praise items, pencils
CLOSING	up to 10	**MAKING PLANS TO PRAISE**—Plan ways to thank and praise God during the coming week.	Paper, pencils
🕑 **FOR EXTRA TIME**	up to 10	**PRAISE, ANCIENT AND MODERN**—Compare modern praise songs to the biblical pattern of praise.	Copies of praise songs and hymns, pencils, paper
	up to 5	**COURSE REFLECTION**—Complete sentences to describe what they've learned from this course.	

The Power of Praise

(up to 10 minutes)

Say: **One of the magnificent things about God is that we can talk with him honestly at all times and in every situation.** Ask someone to read aloud **James 5:13.** Then say: **According to James, we are free to tell God how we feel and to ask him to meet our needs when life is hard. But James also says we should praise God when life is good. Let's begin today's discussion of praise by talking about times people have thanked or praised us.**

Have people turn to partners and each describe a time someone thanked or praised them when they didn't expect it. Allow several minutes for discussion, then invite people to relate their stories to the rest of the class. After several people tell their stories, ask the entire class the following questions:

● **How did it feel to be unexpectedly thanked or praised?**

● **How did this affect your relationship with that person?**

● **How do you think God feels when we praise or thank him?**

● **How can thanks and praise affect our relationship with God?**

T H E P O I N T ▷

Say: **It's much easier to understand why we should praise God than to know how God wants to be praised. So today we're going to discuss how ▷ we honor God with honest praise and open thanks.**

T E A C H E R **TIP**

If you don't want to bake cookies, you can buy and serve a mix of dietetic cookies and regular cookies. However, make sure that the dietetic cookies look as appetizing as the regular ones.

□ **O P T I O N 1 :**

The Right Ingredients

(25 to 35 minutes)

Before class, bake two sets of cookies, one according to the recipe and one without a necessary ingredient such as sugar. Make enough cookies according to the recipe so everyone in the class can have at least one. Make half as many defective cookies. Prepare two pitchers of soft drink mix, one according to directions and one without sugar.

To begin, set out napkins, cups, the two pitchers of drinks, and a plate of each set of cookies. Then say: **When** it's right, praise is something that we enjoy and that God savors. So let's all share some refreshments to symbolize our enjoyment of God's goodness.

Ask for volunteers to help serve the refreshments. Make sure both pitchers and plates of cookies are served. Encourage everyone to accept a cookie and a drink, though it's OK if someone takes only one or the other. Allow people several minutes to eat and drink their refreshments—and to discover that some people received unpalatable refreshments.

Then have people form groups of four. Instruct group members to discuss the following questions. After each question, ask for volunteers to report their groups' answers to the rest of the class. Ask:

- **What's your response to the refreshments you were served?**

- **What makes some of the refreshments better than others?**

- **How are these refreshments like the praises we offer God? How are they different?**

- **What are the essential ingredients of praise that pleases God?**

While groups are discussing the preceding question, hang a sheet of newsprint where everyone can see it. When groups report their answers, write them on the newsprint. After you've listed all the ingredients of praise, serve good cookies and drinks to anyone who would like them.

Say: **Praise that pleases God is always honest and meaningful. It arises from our hearts and our minds. We supply the attitude of praise, always speaking honestly to God from the heart, while God helps us with the act of praise by providing biblical patterns of praise and thanks that we can follow.**

Direct people to read **Psalm 30:1-12** in their groups. While they are reading, write the following questions on a sheet of newsprint and hang it where everyone can see it.
- For what actions does the psalmist praise God?
- What do these actions reveal about God's character?
- To whom does the psalmist address his words?
- What does this imply about the purpose of praise?
- What does this psalm teach about the act of praise?

Tell people they have 10 minutes to discuss the questions in their groups.

When time is up, ask for volunteers to summarize their groups' insights for the rest of the class. Then have the entire class review the ingredients of praise you listed earlier and modify the list to reflect their new understanding

TEACHER
TIP

To avoid wasting any drink, bring sugar to class and add it to the pitcher and cups lacking it.

of praise and thanks.

Say: **To please God, praise needs the right ingredients. It should flow from a sincere heart, and it should be expressed in meaningful words that remind us and everyone around us of who God is and what he's done for his people.**

Then instruct people to form pairs to discuss the following questions. Ask:

- **Which ingredients are sometimes lacking in your praise or thanks?**

- **How do you think God feels about the praise and thanks you offer him?**

- **What can you do to make sure your praise has the essential ingredients?**

- **What will be the benefits of offering God honest praise and open thanks?**

Say: **God enjoys honest praise and open thanks just as much as we enjoy our favorite foods and drinks. However, when one or more of the essential ingredients is missing, it's just not the same. So let's make sure we fully engage our hearts and our minds as ▷we honor God with honest praise and open thanks.**

T H E   P O I N T ▷

■ ■

For *Even Deeper*
Discussion

Form groups of four or fewer to discuss the following questions:

- To what extent should we praise and thank God when we can't do it sincerely? Is it more important to honor God or to be honest with God? How should we pray when we don't feel like praising or thanking God?

- To what extent should we try to create an attitude of praise when we don't feel like praising? How can we develop an attitude of praise without manufacturing false emotions?

■ ■

□ **O p t i o n   2 :**
Personalizing Praise
(30 to 40 minutes)

Before class, make one photocopy of the "Praise, Biblical Style" handout (p. 61) for each class member.

Set out a number of different items people can use to praise God. For example, you might set out paper, pencils, markers, bells, kazoos, party horns, tambourines, spoons, scarves, ribbons, and sticks.

Instruct people to form groups of four. Tell people they have five minutes to plan a 30-second expression of praise to God. Each person should choose his or her own means of praising and then coordinate that expression of praise with those of his or her group members.

After five minutes, have groups take turns presenting their expressions of praise. Encourage people to applaud (and praise!) the efforts of each group. When all groups have expressed their praise to God, have group members discuss the following questions. After each question, ask for volunteers to report their groups' responses to the rest of the class. Ask:

- **What was most natural about praising God? What was most difficult?**

- **To what extent were the different means of praise all valid? of equal value?**

- **What does your means of praising God reveal about your view of praise?**

- **What might happen if everyone chose the same way to praise God?**

Say: **Praise honors God most when it involves our entire selves, when we engage our emotions and enthusiastically praise God and also employ our minds to praise God in a meaningful way. God shows us how to praise him meaningfully in hymns such as Psalm 113.**

Give everyone a copy of the "Praise, Biblical Style" handout and a pencil. Tell people to follow the instructions at the top of the handout. After 10 minutes, encourage people to begin the bottom section of the handout if they haven't already done so.

Give people five more minutes, then ask for volunteers to report their groups' insights about **Psalm 113.** After every group has reported, instruct group members to discuss the following questions. Ask:

- **How well did our earlier praise follow the biblical pattern?**

- **In what ways might we improve our expressions of praise?**

- **What specifically can you do to praise God in a biblical way?**

Then have people spend one minute praising God in whatever way they find most meaningful. Encourage people to focus on God's goodness and good actions on their

God's character and deeds are so closely related that, although they can be distinguished, they cannot be divided. God's character determines what he does, while his actions reveal who he is. There is perfect harmony between the theoretical (God's character) and the experiential (God's actions). Consequently, praise should exalt God both for who he is and for what he does.

behalf. After one minute, say: **We can praise God in our own unique ways as long as we praise him with our entire selves. When we follow the biblical pattern of praising God with our hearts and our minds, ▷ we honor God with the honest praise and open thanks that pleases him most.**

T H E   P O I N T ▷

■ ■

FOR *Even Deeper*
DISCUSSION

Form groups of four or fewer to discuss the following questions:

● Since God reveals his character through his actions, to what extent can we base our ideas about God on our personal experiences? What are the dangers of doing this? What are the benefits? How can we avoid forming incorrect ideas about God?

● What's the proper relationship between private worship and public worship? What are the primary contributions of private worship? of public worship?

■ ■

Apply·It·To·Life™
This Week!

The "Apply-It-To-Life This Week!" handout (p. 62) helps people further explore the issues uncovered in today's class. Give everyone a photocopy of the handout. Encourage class members to take time during the coming week to explore the questions and activities on the handout.

CLOSING

Making Plans to Praise

(up to 10 minutes)

Say: **At times we limit our expressions of praise and thanks to acts such as saying a prayer before meals, singing praise songs, or giving a public testimony of God's work in our lives. But praise and thanks are most meaningful when they're a personal and natural part of our daily lives. So let's close today's lesson by planning ways to thank and praise God during the coming week.**

Give everyone a sheet of paper and a pencil. Instruct people to write on the paper something God has given or done for them personally for which they would like to praise or thank him. For example, people might mention physical healing, a new job, healthy kids, a loving spouse, or an answered prayer.

After everyone finishes, instruct group members to share what they wrote with each other. Then have group members brainstorm creative ways to express to God and share with others their thanks and praise for those things. For example, someone appreciative for a new job could take refreshments to share with co-workers, someone thankful for a spouse might create a card telling the spouse what a blessing he or she is, and someone thankful for healthy kids might take them out for pizza or spend an afternoon with them in the park.

After five minutes, invite people to share their ideas with the rest of the class. Then encourage everyone to commit to one idea for thanking or praising God during the coming week.

THE POINT

Say: ▶ **God is most honored and pleased when we offer him honest praise and open thanks as a natural part of our daily lives. During the weeks to come, take time to remind yourself of the good things God has done for you. Then offer God your honest praise and open thanks by inviting others to share in your expression and celebration of God's goodness to you.**

Close the lesson and the course in prayer, thanking God for his constant presence and our complete freedom to approach him in prayer at all times and in every situation.

For Extra Time

PRAISE, ANCIENT AND MODERN

(up to 10 minutes)

Form groups of four. Give groups copies of popular praise songs or hymns, a sheet of paper, and a pencil. Instruct groups to read their songs and to list what the songs say about who God is and what God does.

After five minutes, ask groups to report what they discovered about their songs. Then have group members discuss the following questions:

- **How adequately does this song describe who God is and what he does?**

- **In your opinion, how well does this song promote an attitude of praise?**

- **In what ways does this song follow the biblical pattern of praise?**

- **Based on what you've learned today, how might you improve this song?**

COURSE REFLECTION

(up to 5 minutes) Ask class members to reflect on the four lessons on prayer. Then have them take turns completing the following sentences:

- Something I learned in this course was...
- If I could tell friends about this course, I'd say...
- Something I'll do differently because of this course is...

Please note class members' comments (along with your own) and send them to Adult Curriculum Editor, Group Publishing, Inc., Dept. BK, Box 481, Loveland, CO 80539. We want your feedback so we can make each course we publish better than the last. Thanks!

Praise, Biblical Style

Working with your group members, read Psalm 113 and discuss the following questions. After you complete the top section of the handout, complete the bottom section on your own. You have 15 minutes to complete the entire handout.

- How do verses 1-3 praise God? encourage praise of God?

- What does the psalmist teach us regarding who God is?

- What does the psalmist say regarding what God has done?

- What's the relation between God's character and his acts?

- According to this psalm, what are the elements of praise?

• •

Complete the following section of the handout on your own. After you finish this section, share your answers with at least one other group member.

- What has God done for you that you can thank or praise him for?

- What can you learn about God's character from this?

Apply·It·To·Life™
This Week!

Praying When Life Is Good

We honor God with honest praise and open thanks.

James 5:13;
Psalms 30:1-12;
and 113:1-9

Reflecting on God's Word

Each day this week, read one of the following Scriptures and examine what it teaches about praising and thanking God. Then consider how you can praise God more honestly and openly in your life. List your discoveries in the space under each passage.

Day 1: Ephesians 5:18-21. The Holy Spirit helps us give thanks in every situation.

Day 2: Philippians 4:6-8. We should thank God when we ask him for what we need.

Day 3: Psalm 138:1-8. Praise and thanks may form the basis for new requests.

Day 4: John 4:23-24. God seeks those who worship him in spirit and in truth.

Day 5: Psalm 8:1-9. We praise God for his greatness and his goodness to us.

Day 6: Psalm 148:1-14. All God's creation should praise him in every way.

Beyond Reflection

Begin each day by thinking of some good thing in your life for which you'd like to thank God. Then think about what that good thing teaches you about God. Record your good thing and what it teaches about God on an index card. Carry the card with you during the day as a reminder to praise God honestly and thank God openly for the good things he has done for you.

Fellowship and Outreach Specials

Use the following activities any time you want. You can use them as part of (or in place of) your regular class activities, or you might consider planning a special event based on one or more of the ideas.

Biblical Prayers

To broaden class members' understanding and appreciation of prayer, invite them to join a group devoted to studying prayer in the Bible. Each time you meet, examine a different biblical model or discussion of prayer (for example, 2 Kings 19:15-19; Psalm 51:1-19; Matthew 6:9-13; John 17:1-26; Ephesians 1:15-19; Philippians 1:9-11; or other relevant texts) to discover biblical principles of prayer. Invite people to share prayer requests and answers to prayer. Then end the study portion of the meeting by applying what you've learned in a time of prayer concerning those requests and answers. Conclude the meeting with refreshments and an informal discussion of group members' struggles and successes in their prayer lives.

We're Praying for You

Each month, have your class "adopt" and pray for another class in your church or even another church in your area. Several times during the month, contact a representative of the other group and ask that person to collect any prayer requests that members of the other group would like you to pray for. Then begin your class by sharing the requests and having class members pray for them. Keep track of the requests so you can report answered prayers to the entire class. You may also want to offer your prayer ministry to homeless shelters, food banks, or other local service organizations.

Honoring God Together

After you complete Lesson 4, plan a thanks and praise party and invite the members of another class or your entire church. Use the occasion to show your guests how to honor God with honest praise and open thanks. To do this, ask your class members to decide how they would like to express their individual thanks and praise to God during a fellowship time or a worship time. Coordinate the individual expressions of praise and thanks to include refreshments for people to enjoy and a worship time that will encourage everyone to praise God in a meaningful way. At the end of the party, explain to your guests how sharing good food and honest praise honors and pleases God.

Apply-It-To-Life Together

Create a meeting based on the "Apply-It-To-Life This Week!" handouts from the course. As a part of the meeting, ask volunteers to share what they discovered through each of the handouts. During the meeting, have people choose one or more "Beyond Reflection" activities to complete together. Establish a schedule with goals for the completion of each of the activities they select.

Petitions and Praises

Decorate a bulletin board in your classroom on which members of your class or church can post prayer requests and answers to prayer. Designate half of the bulletin board for requests and half for answered prayers. Place thumbtacks, pencils, and a stack of index cards near the board. Have people write their prayer requests on the index cards and post them on the board. When God answers a prayer, have the person who made the request move the card from the request side of the board to the answer side. Encourage people to pray for others' requests and to praise God for the answers to prayer. Set aside class time to ask God to meet the requests and to thank him for prayers he's already answered.